Baby Tips for Moms and Dads

Baby Tips
for Moms
and Dads

MARGARET QUEEN

FOXGLOVE PRESS

Baby Tips for Moms and Dads by Margaret Queen

 Published by Foxglove Press
1-877-205-1932
© 2006 Foxglove Press

ISBN 1-882959-57-4

Design by Armour&Armour, Nashville, Tennessee
Editorial assistance by Linda Choate

First Edition 2005

You are the bows from which your children as living arrows are sent forth.

Kahlil Gibran (1883–1931)
Author of *The Prophet*

Introduction

Ironically, I began working on this baby book at the same time that I became a grandmother for the first time. My son called us one Saturday afternoon to say that he and his wife were at the hospital and should have a new baby by the end of the day.

He asked, "What do you remember about the day I was born thirty years ago?" My reply was, "How could I ever forget?" This experience is imprinted in my mind forever. The awakening at 4:00 a.m. thinking that I had gas pains, the fifty-mile drive to the hospital, my doctor's almost-late arrival, my husband's concern and attentiveness, our baby's first cry—these things you never forget. And the word "push" took on a new meaning.

I can remember how thrilled we were with this new baby and how filled we were with the joy of where this new adventure would take us.

Baby Tips for Moms and Dads

Now you are embarking on a journey of your own. You'll never know one day what the next day will bring, and that's part of the fun of the adventure. As your baby grows ever more aware of the outside world, you will find yourself celebrating the joy of learning right along with your child.

Before you know it, you'll be writing new chapters of your own family history.

Author Margaret Queen, far left, and contributor
Judy Garrett, far right

A baby is God's way of saying the world should go on.

Carl Sandburg (1878–1931)
Poet

About This Book

Congratulations on the arrival of your new baby. Now what do you do? I hope that these tips will help you along your parenting journey.

There are hundreds of books on the subject of child rearing. My book is an introduction to this subject. It is not meant to be all-inclusive, but it does address many of the questions raised by parents who want to do the best for their baby.

The following information should not interfere with your parent/physician relationship but will merely provide some helpful hints. At any time that you have concerns about your baby's health and development, call your physician or health care provider.

I have slipped in a few of my favorite baby and early childhood stories from our family to illustrate a few points. My friends have endured so many of my stories that they now hold up their fingers beside their faces to tell me how many times they have heard a certain story. A full five fingers means, "Don't ever tell this story again." But I thought a few of these often-told stories warranted repeating here. I have also added tips for child-rearing from many other parents and friends who have had many experiences to pass on.

Your new baby will be one of the greatest joys of your life. I wrote this book to give Mom and Dad some helpful tips to make their journey a little easier. With each passing day you will gain the confidence and knowledge to become warm, loving parents to this new joy in your life. I hope these insights help you find your way along your parenting path.

A baby is a blank check made payable to the human race.

Barbara Christine Seifert

Contents

THE CHALLENGE AHEAD

Home from the Hospital

This is the moment you have been waiting for. As a new parent, this is your day in the sun, and you will be the one to design the best parent plan for your newborn. Good parenting is a constant work-in-progress.

Advice

You are home with your new baby and ready to begin the parenting journey. Mom and Dad will probably receive plenty of parenting advice from family and friends. Every parent you talk to will be telling you just what to do. Listen politely and then take your own path to parenthood. You have to do what is right for you, your child, and your family.

Before I was married I had three theories about raising children. Now I have three children and no theories.

John Wilmont (1647–1680)
Earl of Rochester

The Challenge Ahead

Challenges

Parenting your child is the greatest challenge that you will ever encounter.

Children will test your mettle. But you will discover inner resources that you never thought you had. Once you realize that your mannerisms, temperament, values, and attitudes will be transmitted to and reflected by your child, you will rise to the occasion.

If you see the world as a wonderful, challenging place full of love and goodness to be experienced through your own actions and attitudes, you will convey these feelings to your baby. If you see the world as a threatening, dangerous, and combative experience, you will likewise transmit that outlook on life.

It is your loving approach to the raising of your child—starting with the way you interact with him in good times as well as stressful times—that will determine how your baby develops his own approach to life.

Loving a baby is a circular business, a kind of feedback loop. The more you give the more you get and the more you get the more you feel like giving.

Penelope Leach (1937–)

British psychologist specializing in child development

The Challenge Ahead

Positive, Loving Approach

Psychologists believe that a baby's attitudes are largely determined during the first few years of childhood. Rise to the occasion: Promise yourself that you will have a positive, loving approach to the good as well as to the inevitable difficult times in raising your child.

You may at times need to seek help from friends, grandparents, and professionals for persistent problems. Don't stop learning about parenting: Use every tool at your disposal. There are many helpful resources. Seek them out.

Set Boundaries

As a parent, you will schedule your child's time and make the rules that you want your child to follow. Children are much more secure and happy when they have firm boundaries. Regularity in feeding times, sleep, and daily events is comforting to small children. Your little one will change rapidly, so be prepared from the beginning. Learn what to expect as you child grows and develops.

Baby Tips for Moms and Dads

There will be many happy times, but prepare yourself for a few sleepless nights, runny noses, fevers, crankiness, cuts, and bruises along the way.

Encouragement

Speak to your child in a kind and loving way. Use words of honest praise, encouragement, and hope. Your tone of voice can be gentle and comforting or abrasive and defeating. It is up to you to set the environment you want for newborn and your family.

There is always one moment in childhood when the door opens and lets the future in.

Deepak Chopra (1946–)

New Age philosopher

FAMILY ISSUES

Siblings

If you already have children at home, make sure that you are paying attention to them as well. Your children's first contacts with the new baby, if handled lovingly by Mom and Dad with an attitude of inclusiveness, will be richly rewarding in building family relationships.

Give brothers and sisters some responsibilities appropriate for their ages and abilities so that they feel as if they too are a part of this child-raising process. It will take some extra effort to get them started with tasks that they can handle but you will be pleasantly surprised about how much help they can be to you. Siblings can bring fresh diapers, help participate in preparing meals, organize clothes, or straighten the baby's room.

Your other children need to know that they will have plenty of Mom's and Dad's attention at this

Baby Tips for Moms and Dads

time, too. It is easy for them to feel slighted as they see all of the attention going to the new arrival. Including them in daily processes teaches them that raising the new baby is a family affair and that they are an important part of the family.

Joint Effort

Raising this new little one is a two-person job. If Mom cooks dinner, then Dad needs to do the dishes or help with the cleaning. If Mom is breastfeeding, then Dad can fold laundry or go grocery shopping. This is a time when both Mom and Dad need each other's support.

Children in a family are like flowers in a bouquet; there's always one determined to face in the opposite direction from the way the arranger desires.

Marcelene Cox
American writer

Baby Tips for Moms and Dads

Family Issues

Grandparents

How wonderful for a child to have grandparents! A child growing up with active and vital grandparents is a lucky one. Grandparents normally will want to be included in this new relationship with your baby. There will be some negotiation and adjustment about how to handle the daily routine if they are living close to you.

Re-defining the relationship with your own parents can bring great joy to you all. It is momentous for grandparents to have this new role and worth the effort to develop this valuable resource. Grandparents, however, may be limited by their age and resources and temperament. They may have different ideas on how your children should be raised. Remember that they have raised their own children and are a good source of advice. (After all, you turned out okay.) But you need to make your own decisions.

You have the prime responsibility for your baby, but grandparents can be amazingly helpful. Cultivate this new relationship. They remember how it was and are usually delighted to give you a helping hand. They will be glad to hold a fussy baby or give you a break in cooking a meal, baby-sit while you run to the store, or assist with a load of laundry. Mom and Dad will need a little "time out" time. Who better to rely on for a babysitter than your baby's grandparents?

Grandparents: Remember you are big and they are little; get down on their level, the floor, even if you need help getting up.

Don Garrett M.D.

Father of three, grandfather of ten

Have children while
your parents are still
young enough to
take care of them.

Rita Rudner (1956–)
Comedian

Baby Tips for Moms and Dads

Pictures of Your Baby

Take lots of pictures so that you can send photos to family and friends who can't be there to see your child grow up. We took some wonderful pictures posing our children doing grown-up activities such as sitting behind the driver's wheel looking out the car window in the driveway. Our favorite is our son sitting in the bathtub with his face lathered and shaving in a mirror. (We took the blade out of the razor first!)

Family Issues

When you run into a good friend who asks to see a picture of your new baby, they actually mean **A** picture—just one or two. Grandmas are different; they want to see everything.

We took rolls and rolls of film of our first child. We overdid it so much the first time that we took very few baby pictures of our daughter, who came along three years later. She is still a little irritated that we have so few baby pictures of her.

Purchase a good camera and use it often. Your baby will be a baby for only a very short time, and it is important to capture those moments as often as possible. You will enjoy them later when your baby has grown up. Your child will love to have the pictures to view later, and it helps them know that you really cared for them.

Phil McCowan

Father of two, grandfather of two

Baby Tips for Moms and Dads

Take pictures, pictures, pictures. Date them and label who is in each one. You will be so glad years later. Keep a monthly log of things they did and funny things they said up until age four or five. Then make entries on a yearly basis. Give it to them on a special occasion such as graduation or when they have their first child.

Val Lambert

Mother of two

We worry about what a
child will be tomorrow,
yet we forget that he
is someone today.

Stacia Tauscher

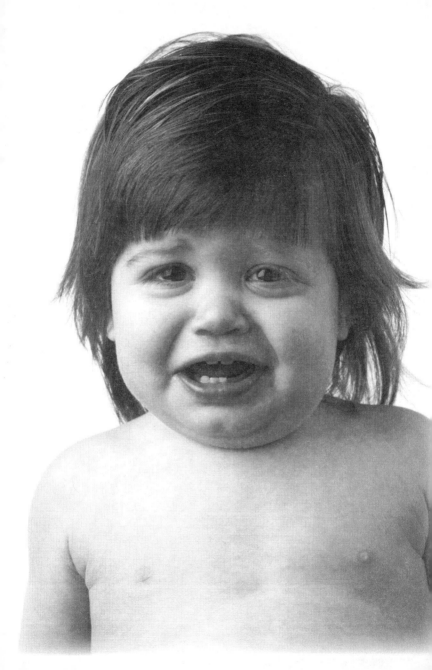

CRYING

How Babies Communicate

Crying is the way babies communicate with their new world. If they could just tell you about their needs, parenthood would be so much easier. Remember that crying is normal. If your baby is crying start with the following checklist to see if you can find out what he wants:

1. Wet or soiled diaper. *Please give me a change.*

2. I'm hungry. *Time for a meal.*

3. I'm too hot or too cold. *Check my clothing.*

4. I'm tired. *I need a nap or to go to bed.*

5. I don't feel well. *Check for fever or other indicators.*

6. I want some attention. *Come pick me up and give me some love.*

7. I have a gas bubble. *Burp me or hold me upright.*

Baby Tips for Moms and Dads

8. I'm lonely. *Sing or talk to me. I love to hear your voice and know you are near.*

9. I could have colic. *I need to be held and soothed.*

Colic is generally described as a newborn's crying for an hour or two a day the first two months of life for no apparent reason and then gradually subsiding. Check in with your physician for some help here. A colicky baby who cries a lot is difficult on Mom and Dad. Be as calm and patient as you can, and know that this stage will pass. This is a good opportunity for Grandma to give you some help during this stressful time.

It is okay for a baby to cry. It is their only way to communicate their pain or displeasure. Try to comfort them and ease their pain but do not expect to prevent or stop all crying.

Sally Hildebrandt
Mother of five, grandmother of three

Crying

It won't be long before you learn the meaning of your baby's cries. The cry of a hungry child is different from the cry of one who is ill or in pain. Listen particularly for the difference in pitch.

If you feel that your baby is crying more than seems normal, give your doctor a call to make sure that there is not an underlying medical problem.

If your baby's crying is getting the best of you and you feel frustrated, put her in bed and step out of the room for a few minutes to collect yourself. This will allow you to gather your patience so you don't have a complete meltdown. If all else fails, try what we discovered: Our children would quit crying as soon as we put them in their carrier and went for a walk.

Mom Can Cry, Too

Remember that it is normal for moms to cry every once in a while too. Being a new mom is hard work; it's easy to get frustrated trying to do too

Baby Tips for Moms and Dads

many things at one time with little time for yourself.

Babies who are excessively cranky, sleep poorly, or spit up a great deal may put a strain on Mom. Throw in the added hormone changes you experience after giving birth, and you may have a case of the "new baby blues." This should pass as your baby begins to sleep through the night and you get adjusted to your new routine and are finally able to get a full night's sleep.

If this does not pass quickly, please share you feelings with your health care provider. Postpartum depression is a serious matter; you may need professional help coping with your feelings.

If your baby's "beautiful and perfect, never cries or fusses, sleeps on schedule and burps on demand, an angel all the time," you're the grandma.

Teresa Bloomingdale
Humorist

Baby Tips for Moms and Dads

Talking

Your baby will begin saying his first words about the age of one year. It is hard to tell when a child makes the transition from mimicking sounds to saying meaningful words. It's normal for this transition to take a long time. Our son was slow to start talking but moved from a few words to complete sentences quickly.

~~~~~~~~~~~~~~~~~~~~~~~~~~~~~~

We had great fun with our children when they began to talk. They loved to make the sounds of the different animals as we looked at pictures in a book. Our kids loved to say "bow wow" for a dog and "cock-a-doodle-do" for a rooster. We were all more than surprised to go through the same animals with a Norwegian cousin who was our son's same age and discover that a Norwegian dog goes "noof noof" and a Norwegian rooster goes "key killy key."

MQ

~~~~~~~~~~~~~~~~~~~~~~~~~~~~~~

Pretty much all the honest truth telling there is in the world is done by children.

Anonymous

FEEDING YOUR BABY

Breastfeeding

I recommend breastfeeding, and more than seventy percent of new mothers agree. The formula companies are spending millions to attempt to duplicate what nature provides just for the asking. Breastfeeding has the following advantages:

1. Mom and her new baby get special time together.

2. Your baby is getting colostrum from his first feedings, which fights off harmful bacteria and stimulates the immune system.

3. You don't have to make and heat a bottle. Everything you need for your baby's meal you have right with you.

4. It's free!

There are three reasons for breastfeeding: the milk is always at the right temperature; it comes in attractive containers; and the cat can't get it.

Irene Chalmers
Cookbook publisher

Feeding Your Baby

Feeding time is a great opportunity to hold your baby close to you. It's a great time to talk to your baby, smile, and sing, if you are so inclined. Feeding time is a great bonding experience between Mom and baby.

Look for a lactation consultant to get you off to a good start.

Get a breast pump so you can express milk into a bottle. That way, you have a bottle of milk in the refrigerator when you are out of the house and Dad or the babysitter needs to feed the little one.

Before feeding, make sure that you wash your hands and your baby's hands to keep from spreading germs.

When feeding, take your time. Babies who eat slowly have less gas. Stop every few minutes, hold your infant to your shoulder and rub or pat his back gently to help any gas bubbles subside. Make sure that his head is supported. You may need to change positions if you are not successful with this at first. Your baby may bring up a little milk with his gas bubble, so put a cloth over your shoulder to make clean-up easier.

The more your baby breastfeeds, the more milk you will produce. Make sure that you begin the next feeding with the opposite breast. It will take a few weeks to determine the feeding routine that works best for your baby. Feeding more often than every two hours is inefficient. As your baby grows, the intervals between feedings lengthen as the baby drinks more milk. Since every baby is different in terms of size, maturity, and temperament, it is best to discuss details about feeding schedules with your physician.

Breastfeeding in public has become much more acceptable in this country. If you are shy about this, make a tent over your baby with a small blanket so you can feed your baby in the company of friends and family without thinking you are exposing yourself. If you have an abundance of milk, you might put some pads in your bra to absorb any leaks.

Feeding Your Baby

You may need to supplement your breastfeeding with formula if you do not produce enough milk. My son was just not getting enough breast milk, so I had to add formula almost immediately.

Formula

Some mothers cannot or prefer not to breastfeed. That's okay, too. You'll find several good formulas

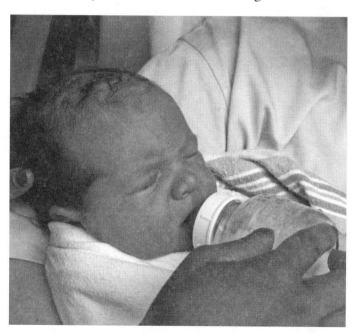

Baby Tips for Moms and Dads

on the market—ask your physician for a recommendation. Check the can of formula at the store to make sure that it is not out of date and then follow the manufacturer's directions for preparing your baby's formula.

You can make up bottles ahead of time and keep them in the refrigerator. Throw away any unused formula from a feeding; start each feeding with a fresh bottle of formula.

Make sure that you sterilize your bottles and nipples. You will need to use a bottle brush to remove any residue from inside the bottle.

Formula feeding does have some advantages:

1. You can measure exactly how many ounces of milk your baby has consumed.
2. Dad or another family member can feed your baby.
3. You can easily leave a bottle for the babysitter when you go out.

There is no finer investment for any community than putting milk into babies.

Winston Churchill (1874-1965)

British prime minister

Baby Tips for Moms and Dads

Introducing Solid Food

Breast milk or formula is a newborn's primary food for the first several months of life. As your baby matures, if she still seems to be hungry after regular feedings it may be time to introduce some rice cereal. Ask your physician for his recommendation.

When your baby is ready for solid food, that means home cooking with ground food or commercial foods. Always read the ingredients of commercial baby foods: The first item listed is the main ingredient. Your physician can provide information on how to prepare home-cooked foods and a recommended sequence for starting foods.

Cup Training

Start around six months with water or juice. With some practice your child will soon be able to take liquids this way. As your baby continues to grow, encourage water as opposed to soft drinks or high-sugar drinks or any drink with caffeine.

We can see that the baby is as much an instrument of nourishment for us as we are for him.

Polly Berrien Berends
Author

Baby Tips for Moms and Dads

Good Nutritional Habits

The move to solid food is the time to introduce good eating habits that will stay with your child for a lifetime. This is your chance to give your children a firm nutritional foundation.

Begin with cereals and vegetables. As your child begins to eat more variety, stay away from sweets, fast foods, fried food, and pre-prepared foods. We have become a nation of overweight adults, and children are quickly becoming part of this group. Even children are "super sizing" their meals. Good eating habits, started in early childhood, are the best defense against health risks such as diabetes, which has become a national health threat.

How Much is Enough?

As you start providing solid food, your child will give you a clue as to how much food is enough. Every child is different, but in general, hungry babies lean forward, are very focused, and follow that spoon. When full, they begin to lean back, look around, and play; they may even turn their heads away from the spoon. This is a good indication that your baby is telling you, "I am full."

Healthy Snacks

Once your child is old enough to be eating table foods, you will be giving your little ones snacks between meals. There are so many healthy snacks that you can give your children. Children love cut-up vegetables, chunks of fresh fruit, crackers, cheese, small pretzel sticks, and Cheerios. Keep a small sealable bag of crackers and bottled water in the car. You just never know when you might need them. Instead of a soda, we gave our children the mini-cans of fruit juice. For special treats we bought small bottles of sparkling apple juice. This was a good as a Coke to them. They don't drink soft drinks now as adults, and they have far fewer cavities than their parents.

Eating with the Family

Socialization begins when your baby can sit in a high chair and eat with the rest of the family.

Baby Tips for Moms and Dads

It is important that you use good table manners as a lead for your child to follow. Remember, as your children become more socialized, they also begin to understand and say back some of your words. Keep your conversation G-rated. Remember that your words may be repeated in front of the preacher or family friend or grandparents at an inopportune time.

Children seldom misquote you. In fact, they usually repeat word for word what you should not have said.

Author Unknown

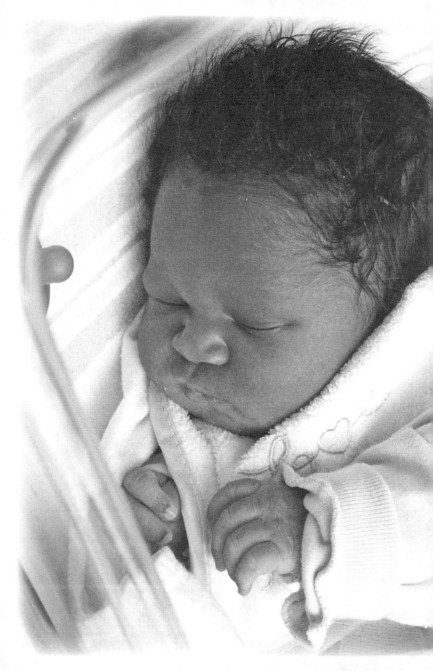

SLEEPING

Sleep

Babies sleep a lot the first few weeks. The problem is that they often sleep during the day and then get hungry and stay awake in the middle of the night. Use a rocking chair for these middle-of-the-night feedings. Keep the lights dimmed and put your baby back to bed after feeding.

As your baby gets older and can eat more at a feeding, he will begin to awaken less in the middle of the night. Your baby should begin to sleep through the night by two to four months of age.

Babies should have their own place to sleep. Don't let your child sleep with you; it is a hard habit to break. Once your baby is sleeping in his own room, use a monitor so that you can know when he awakens.

Babies need to be put to bed on their backs.

People who say that they sleep like a baby usually don't have one.

Leo J. Burke

Sleep

If your baby does wake in the night and you are sure that all needs have been met, it is okay to let him cry for a while. Often babies hear a noise and come only partially awake; they will soon settle down and go back to sleep.

Bedtime

Bedtime is an individual decision, but unless they are over-stimulated, babies generally follow the rhythm of nature: They begin tiring at dusk and are ready for sleep by darkness. Put your baby to bed around the same time each night and develop a bedtime ritual—such as singing a lullaby, saying a prayer, or reading a book—to help bring sleep.

Begin the ritual with a bath and some quiet time. This becomes your baby's special time with his parents. You should plan on taking at least half an hour to get your baby bathed and quiet for sleeping.

Don't let your child become over-tired because it is often harder to get to sleep. Learn the sleep pattern that works best for your child.

Baby Tips for Moms and Dads

Routine

Babies are happier with a routine. If they eat at about the same time each day, take a nap, and get enough sleep, they will be well-fed and rested— and Mom and Dad will see how much more enjoyable they are to be around.

I am always amazed to see a family out having dinner at eight p.m. or even later. Their baby is cranky, and everyone at the table is miserable. If you're eating late, stay home or get a babysitter.

With young children, the first thing is always sleep and blood sugar. Nothing else you do to encourage or discipline a child will be effective if your child isn't well-rested and well-fed. Protect your child's sleep like a tigress, and don't leave home without crackers and cheese sticks.

Donya Rose
Mother of four

Sleep

My dad was the storyteller at my house before bedtime. He used to make up a new story every night about a little boy named Charlie Nosewiper who lived at the firehouse. Charlie went to a fire every night in the fireman's coat pocket. On occasions my mother would pinch-hit at story time, but I used to get so mad at her because every time she would fall asleep before getting to the end of the story. Now I can understand why she was so tired.

MQ

Afraid of the Dark

Some children don't like to go to bed in a dark room. A night light will help them feel more secure. I often left the hall light on with their door open, which allowed plenty of indirect light in their room.

Baby Tips for Moms and Dads

Sleep for Mom and Dad

For a while, Mom will have difficulty getting enough sleep. Babies need to be fed during the night for the first few months, which means that your sleep will be interrupted constantly during this time. When your baby is sleeping during the day, Mom should take an afternoon nap to get her through the nightly feedings.

One of your greatest joys comes when your baby begins to sleep through the night. Mom and Dad finally get a full night's sleep, and life becomes so much less stressful.

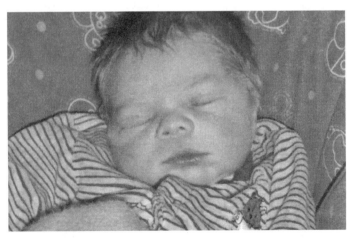

Insomnia: A contagious disease often transmitted from babies to parents.

Shannon Fife

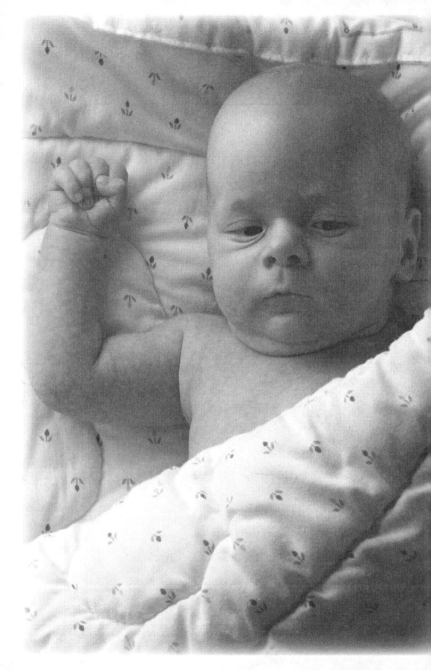

CLEANUP

Diaper Change

Check your baby's diaper often to see if it is wet or soiled. Never stick your finger into your baby's diaper to see if it needs to be changed. You might get an unwanted surprise!

You can never have too many diapers. Keep lots of extra plastic bags to wrap the dirty diapers in before putting them in the trash. This will keep your baby's room from stinking.

Changing the diaper of little boys can be a challenge. Somehow the feeling of fresh air on his skin as you remove his diaper stimulates him to let go. Be careful where you are changing his diaper so that this little fountain doesn't spray you or your best furniture.

Never leave home without your diaper changing equipment. You may think that you will just

Baby Tips for Moms and Dads

run in the store for a quick minute. That will be the time you need a clean diaper the most. Bring plenty of supplies: moist wipes, extra diapers, rash ointment, extra plastic disposal bags, and the works.

Don't wake your baby to change a wet diaper, only when he has had a bowel movement.

Make sure that you wash your hands well after every diaper change.

~~~~~~~~~~~~~~~~~~~~~~~~

Our worst ever need for a diaper change came at a fancy Chinese restaurant packed with guests. It had been eleven years since we had seen our friends, a member of our wedding party and his wife. I held our fussy daughter while my husband ate his dinner. As soon as I handed off our daughter to my husband, she literally exploded in his lap. We had to wrap her

Cleanup

in white linen napkins, and my husband carried her as he elbowed his way through the crowd to the door. I followed him to the car where we laid our daughter in the open trunk and wrapped her in newspapers. We then got into the car, holding her—as well as our breath—in the backseat all the way back to our friend's house. Our daughter had to be hosed down in the yard before we could even go inside and give her a real bath. I don't think I ever ate my dinner that night. And our friends never did have children.

MQ

Diaper Rash

A diaper rash is so easy to begin and so hard to get rid of. This is one place where an ounce of prevention goes a long way. Generally, good hygiene with frequent diaper changes is all that is necessary to prevent diaper rashes. Make sure you

Baby Tips for Moms and Dads

clean your baby thoroughly with a warm washrag or diaper wipe. Let your baby go without a diaper for a few minutes every day. This gives the skin a chance to dry out.

Diaper rashes are much less common since the introduction of disposable diapers. Yet baby wipes can cause rashes in infants with sensitive skin. Changing brands may be helpful. There are many anti-diaper rash remedies over the counter that can protect your baby's skin from moisture or a soiled diaper until the rash heals. Keep some of this medication handy; you usually need it when it is least handy to run to the store.

If your baby seems to have constant diaper rashes, try another brand of diapers. Your baby may have an allergy to a particular brand. If this doesn't work, consult your physician.

While we teach our children all about life, our children teach us what life is all about.

Anonymous

Baby Tips for Moms and Dads

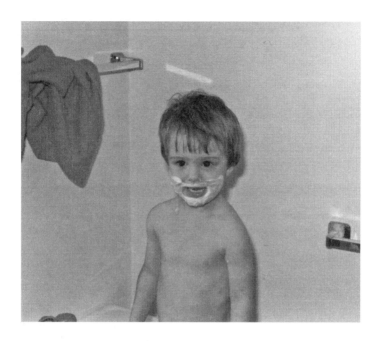

Bathing

This should be a fun experience for both of you.
Babies love to play in the water. You can begin
a full bath as soon as the navel and circumcision
have healed. I found it best to bathe my babies before I put them to bed. A warm bath is soothing,
and your baby will have a relaxed, quiet time with
you before bedtime. A few tips to remember:

Cleanup

1. Check the temperature of the water before you put the baby in the bath. My mother used to test the temperature with her elbow, which is more sensitive than hands or fingers. The room for bathing should be warm: Don't have a fan or air conditioning blowing.

2. Remember that a wet baby is a slippery baby. Hang on with both hands when putting her in and out of the bath.

3. Never leave the baby alone in the bath.

4. Very young babies need to have their heads supported.

5. You don't have to give a full bath every day: A good sponge bath will suffice.

6. You don't need to shampoo every day. When you do, make sure you use a tearless shampoo.

7. Wash the face, chest, and hands first while the wash cloth is clean. Bathe your baby's bottom last. Be thorough.

8. Little boys can spray you at this time as well. Be alert.

Baby Tips for Moms and Dads

Once your baby can hold his head up he may enjoy bathing with either Mom or Dad—and you
will, too. At this time, add a few water toys to
make this event more fun.

Children require guidance and sympathy far more than instruction.

Anne Sullivan (1866–1936)

Helen Keller's teacher

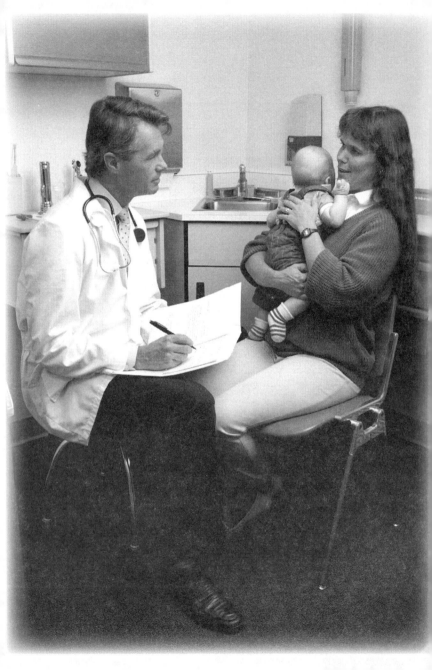

HEALTH AND SAFETY

Physician

I hope you have chosen a physician with whom you are comfortable, one you can look upon as a wise teacher and trusted guide. Your doctor will be there for you: to help you along the way with well-baby checkups as well as when you need advice about your baby's illnesses or problems. Keep your physician's phone number handy.

Checkups

Follow the checkup schedule recommended by your physician. The doctor will keep an eye on growth, development, proper nutrition, and behavior, and check on your parental concerns. Babies change so rapidly that discovering problems quickly is essential for proper medical intervention. Ask your doctor for recommendations for your baby's immunizations.

Baby Tips for Moms and Dads

Check these indicators to see if your child is ill:

1. Does your child have a fever?
2. Has the child had a change in sleeping habits?
3. How is your child's appetite?
4. Is there a change in temperament?
5. Is there a change in activity level?

If any of these indicators persist, give your physician a call.

Fever

Fever is a friend that helps the body rally forces to wipe out the invading illness. To take your child's temperature, use a simple digital thermometer (not mercury). An axillary (under the arm) measurement is satisfactory. Some parents who frequently take their infant's temperature sometimes discover a fever with no apparent cause—in reality, the baby is covered with too many blankets or too much clothing. How aggressively to manage fevers is best discussed with your physician.

Health and Safety

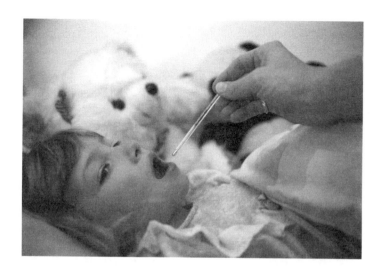

My Mom's Food Remedies When I Was Sick

My mom had a routine for trying to eat after an upset stomach. Food was introduced in the following order:

1. Soda crackers with 7Up
2. If that stayed down, move to chicken noodle soup.
3. Toast, no jelly
4. Hot cereal

Baby Tips for Moms and Dads

She would put a bell next to my bed that I could ring when I needed her.

A Parent's Tool Box

1. Physician's phone number
2. Phone number for the National Poison Control Center (800-222-1222 twenty-four hours a day)
3. You never have too many diapers.
4. Tylenol drops or equivalent
5. Diaper rash cream
6. Digital thermometer
7. A nose syringe. Don't overuse—most infants hate them.
8. Cold remedy recommended by your physician
9. A syringe that accurately measures in millimeters or cubic centimeters.
10. Antibiotic ointment such as Neosporin
11. Cool mist vaporizer

Health and Safety

12. Camera ready for those precious moments

13. Baby book and baby diary

14. Plastic bags in the car, in your diaper bag, or anyplace in the house where you might need to dispose of a dirty diaper. You can't have too many plastic bags.

Sudden Infant Death Syndrome

Known as SIDS, this is considered to be an unexpected death from a normally healthy baby with no apparent reason. Any time you see the word *syndrome*, you know the cause is unknown. So what can a parent do? Here are some suggestions:

1. Put your child to sleep on his back. Make sure that all of your babysitters and day care personnel are instructed to do this.

2. Don't put stuffed animals or blankets around your baby; they can get up over her head. A one-piece sleeping garment is ideal. If you are covering your baby with a blanket at night for sleeping, put the feet all the way to the bottom of the crib. Tuck the blanket

in at the bottom and bring it up under the arms so that it is impossible to pull over the head.

3. Don't smoke.

4. Don't over-dress your baby for sleeping. Make sure that he is not over-heated.

Exposure to the Sun

Newborn babies and infants are very susceptible to the sun and get burned much more quickly than older people. When you take your baby out for a walk, she needs to be shaded from the sun with a cover on the stroller or a light-colored hat and clothing. Make every attempt when outdoors to keep your baby in the shade, but even that is not totally safe.

Sunscreen

Begin using sunscreen when your child is more than six months old. Use a sunscreen with a SPF (sun proof factor) of at least fifteen or higher. Sunscreen can be an irritant and cause a rash on young babies. You can test it by putting a small amount on your baby's arm to see if he has any reaction to it.

Bug in the Ear

If your child has a insect in his ear, here is an easy remedy for what can be a frightening situation. Turn your child's head to the side and pour in lots of water, and the insect will be flushed out.

For a calming effect, your newborn will love this. Put a ticktock clock near the bed. Your little one will think he/she is listening to mother's heartbeat.

Janice Feldman

Reducing Stress for Mom and Dad

Usually the greatest stress on new parents is exhaustion and the all-consuming responsibility of their new baby.

Baby Tips for Moms and Dads

Here are some helpful tips.

1. Take a nap yourself when your baby is sleeping.

2. After your baby has gone to bed at night take an hour for yourself. Have some quality quiet time, read, write in a journal, work on a craft project, but take a few minutes every day for yourself.

3. Have your spouse take responsibility for your baby for a few hours every week so that you can leave the house alone. You might meet a friend for coffee or even just go to the store alone.

4. You and your baby can take an exercise or swim class together. You both are out of the house together doing things with other parents to talk to. These classes are usually available at your community center or the YMCA.

5. Don't plan too many social events or have too many visitors for the first few months. It is easier to establish a routine with your child without too many visitors.

If you bungle raising your children, I don't think whatever else you do matters.

Jacqueline Kennedy Onassis (1930–1994)
First Lady of the United States

Baby Tips for Moms and Dads

Keep a comfortable chair and a book for you in the baby's room or near the play space. Sometimes your baby or toddler just wants reassurance that someone is near, and you get a break, too.

Janice Feldman

A Night Out for Mom and Dad

Mom and Dad need to have a date night and get away from the house at least once a month. Plan ahead for your date and find a good babysitter. Make these dates special occasions. You both need some special time just to connect with each other. Set a regular date night and put it on your calendar.

Teething

Teething usually begins at four to six months of age. You'll know when your baby starts teething by the aggressive tendency to gum any object

Trust yourself.
You know more
than you think
you do.

Dr. Benjamin Spock (1903–1998)

Authority on child rearing

Baby Tips for Moms and Dads

your child can put in his mouth, especially hands. You may see a slight increase in fussiness and night-time wakening. Giving your baby a teething ring to chew on can be helpful.

Babies seem to drool excessively when they are teething. This is a good time to keep a bib on your baby to keep the front of his clothing dry. This teething phase will pass.

We had an episode lasting a few days when our son was excessively fussy when he was teething. I finally went to my mom's remedy of rubbing a few drops of whiskey on his gums. It seemed to help with his pain.

MQ

You should begin brushing your baby's teeth or wiping with a soft cloth as soon as his first tooth appears.

Adam and Eve had many advantages, but the principle one was that they escaped teething.

Mark Twain (1835–1910)

Author and humorist

Baby Tips for Moms and Dads

Health and Safety

Out for a Walk

You will enjoy parenthood more if you get out of the house occasionally. Your baby will especially enjoy an outing while being carried in a front carrier or in a sling. The change of scenery, the fresh air, and the exercise is great for the both of you.

Be sure to dress your baby a little more warmly than you are dressed, because you are exercising more than your baby and generating more heat. Babies need some type of head covering, as most have little or very thin hair to keep their heads warm.

Exercise

As your children begin to walk, take them outside. Create a fun, safe play environment for them outside.

Children need the exercise and a chance to explore their environment. Your child will sleep much better at night if he has some exercise during the day.

Baby Tips for Moms and Dads

As our son began to walk, I put him in a harness with a lead strap so that we could walk more freely and safely, and I could hold him back from stepping into dangerous places. I felt that this was so much easier for us both to navigate busy sidewalks, and I could restrain him from darting out into traffic. I received a few smart remarks from by passers-by about my child on a leash as if I were inhumane, but we both liked it and were a lot safer.

MQ

What feeling is as nice as a child's hand in yours? So small, so soft and so warm, like a kitten huddling in the shelter of your grasp.

Marjorie Holmes (1910–2002)
Writer

Baby Tips for Moms and Dads

Safety Tips

1. Put safety tops (available at any hardware store) on electrical outlets. Outlets are at a crawling baby's level and are an open invitation to an inquisitive finger or a toy.

2. Put cabinet locks on all of your lower cabinets.

3. Baby-proof the house so that all medications, household cleansers, or anything that might be harmful are out of reach or locked in a cabinet.

4. Turn down the water heater so that the baby's bath is not too hot.

5. Police floors and tables constantly. It's amazing what babies can find and put in their mouths.

6. Teach your child how to climb and descend stairs. Keep toys off stairs!

7. Keep syrup of ipecac and activated charcoal on hand and learn how to use them.

9. Sign up at your hospital for the Red Cross training for infant and child CPR.

Health and Safety

10. Make sure that your house has a working smoke alarm and carbon monoxide detector. Change batteries when Daylight Saving Time begins and ends.

11. Never allow your child to play with a plastic bag.

12. Don't leave your baby alone with a young child or a family pet. Very young children don't yet know how to treat the new addition to your household, and your pet could bite or scratch if the baby pulls on it or startles it.

13. Don't leave your baby in a carseat or carrier on a counter or other high places. Babies wiggle a lot and can overturn the carrier. It is long drop from the kitchen counter.

14. Never leave your baby or young child alone in the car, even just for a minute. Too many bad things can happen even if it is not a hot day.

Baby Tips for Moms and Dads

We have good friends who left their eighteen-month-old son in a car with the motor running. He climbed out of his carseat, got behind the steering wheel, and put the car in gear. The car jumped the curb and hit the window of the dry cleaner where his mom was picking up clothes. Who would have imagined, but it can happen.

MQ

Make sure that your baby cannot play with any kind of string or cord—telephone cord, electric cord, curtain tie, or drapery pull—that might wrap around his neck.

Once your child is crawling, he can get into everything. It only takes a second for babies to get into something they should not. Prevention is definitely the best answer here. A crawling baby can pull the end of a tablecloth and have plates or hot coffee fall on him.

Health and Safety

We had stopped to visit an older couple for a few minutes. Our two-year-old son was with us. He disappeared into their bedroom for just a few seconds, then appeared with a half-eaten pill drooling from his mouth. It was a nitroglycerine tablet from a bedside table, kept in a small, inviting bottle easily in reach of a child. We spent the rest of the evening talking with the Poison Control Center and watching our son for any unusual symptoms.

MQ

Curiosity

Babies are naturally curious. Your baby has a new world of people, places, and things to learn about. They want to touch and grab everything within their reach. Most items they can pull to themselves go right to their mouth for a taste test. As they begin to crawl they will be into everything.

I think at a child's birth, if a mother could ask a fairy godmother to endow it with the most unusual gift, that gift should be curiosity.

Eleanor Roosevelt (1884–1962)

First Lady of the United States

Health and Safety

We have a favorite story about my son's experiment with his environment when he was eighteen months old. I had stepped outside for a few moments while he was playing on the kitchen floor. As soon as I closed the door behind me, he opened the refrigerator and pulled a nearly full gallon of milk onto the floor. He proceeded to take off all of his clothes and put them where they would not get wet. Then he poured the gallon of milk on the floor and was swimming naked in the milk having a great time when I looked back inside. I remember well sitting in the floor crying as I tried to figure out how I was going to clean up this mess.

MQ

Baby Tips for Moms and Dads

Our daughter had just gotten out of the tub. I was drying her off in our bedroom on our fine oriental rug and was about to dry her hair when the phone rang. From the kitchen I could hear our daughter turn on the dryer and begin to dry her hair all by herself. Soon I heard this terrible grinding sound of the hair dryer and imagined her long hair being somehow consumed. As I reached the bedroom door I was quite amazed to see our daughter standing over the hair dryer urinating into it as it made this horrible noise. I quickly pulled the power cord with great relief that she did not receive an electric shock. Needless to say, we bought a new dryer. The oriental rug is fine and on my bedroom floor to this day.

MQ

We are always too busy for our children, we never give them the time or interest they deserve. We lavish gifts upon them, but the most precious gift—our personal association which means so much to them—we give grudgingly.

Mark Twain (1835-1910)
Author and humorist

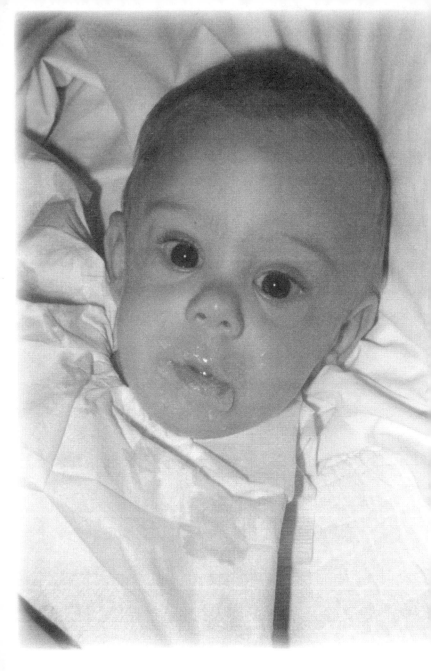

DISCIPLINE

Here are some tips on guiding your child's behavior:

1. Start with a loving attitude toward your child's discipline.

2. Be a good example in the way you deal with anger and frustrations.

3. Be consistent in your rules and expectations.

4. Mean what you say. Don't give in when your child complains and cries, as he will think that this is how he gets what he wants the next time.

5. Bring your child into the rule formulation process. Ask, "What do you think is fair?"

6. If you need to discipline your child, try not to do this in a room full of family and friends. Take her aside and talk. Criticism is hard enough for your child to take; receiving criticism in front of others can be devastating.

7. Don't lose your temper. If you feel over-

whelmed by the situation, leave the room and collect yourself.

~~~~~~~~~~~~~~~~~~~~~~~~~~

My advice for parents of young children is to take the time to think before you give your child an answer that contains "no" . . . then don't change your mind. "No" becomes more valuable after a while.

Donna Senior
Mother of three

~~~~~~~~~~~~~~~~~~~~~~~~~~

Find ways to discipline your child other than spanking. My favorite method is to give the child a "time out" in instances of inappropriate behavior. Just remove the child from the situation, take a deep breath, and realize this, too, will pass.

Disciplining your child will be one of your greatest challenges. Just remember that this is a time for patience on your part: Be forgiving for their mistakes, and practice unconditional love. Children and parents can both make mistakes.

Any child can tell you
that the sole purpose
of a middle name is so
he can tell whether
he's in trouble.

Dennis Fakes

Don't discipline in anger. Wait until you can explain calmly what the infraction of rules was, and what the consequence will be. And then make sure that the punishment fits the crime.

Judy Dancy

An apology

When you have made a mistake or over-reacted to your child's behavior, an apology is in order (if your child is old enough to understand). This is an amazing thing that parents rarely do. (Teachers could learn this one, too.) Children need to know that their parents are not perfect and can make a mistake too.

They appreciate honesty from you. This works wonders as your children get older. Children realize that they are not the only ones who make mistakes. It makes them feel important that their parents need their forgiveness.

A torn jacket is soon mended, but hard words bruise the heart of a child.

Henry Wadsworth Longfellow (1807–1882)

Poet

Baby Tips for Moms and Dads

Children are not miniature adults. Their minds, bodies, and spirits are just developing. They need love, nurture, guidance, and protection from their parents.

Children thrive on structure and boundaries. They may fight against them at times but, just like a warm blanket wrapped around them, they love the security and safety of knowing that a strong adult is in charge. Say "yes" to your children whenever possible. Don't be afraid, however, to say "no" when the request is not safe. Don't take a child's misbehavior personally. The issue is not you or your parenting skills. It is easier to deal rationally with misbehavior if you can separate your ego from the problem.

Sally Hildebrandt
Mother of five, grandmother of three

Good parents give their children roots and wings: roots to know where home is, wings to fly away and exercise what's been taught them.

Jonas Salk *(1914–1995)*
Developer of the polio vaccine

Baby Tips for Moms and Dads

Don't ever lie. If they ask about whether a shot will hurt, it is better to tell them that it will sting for a minute but that you will be there with them. If you lie to them about small things, they will not trust you to tell them the truth about the big things.

Sally Hildebrandt
Mother of five, grandmother of three

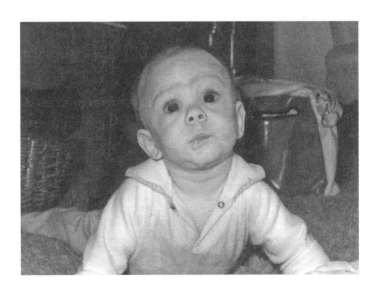

It is not giving children more that spoils them, it is giving them more to avoid confrontation.

John Gray (1951–)

Author of *Men are from Mars, Women Are from Venus*

EQUIPMENT

Carseats

These are a must as well as required by law. When choosing a carseat be sure that it meets Federal Motor Vehicle Safety Standards. Small babies should begin riding in the back seat facing the rear of the car.

Make sure that your seat is the right size for the weight and size of your baby. Follow the manufacturer's directions for securing your child in the carseat and attaching the carseat to your car.

You will need to take your child's carseat along if you travel and need to take a commercial cab. It is illegal for a child to ride in a cab without being belted into a legal child carseat. You will need the carseat for a ride in any car, no matter whom your family travels with.

Baby Tips for Moms and Dads

Rocking chair

Babies love to be held and rocked. They were rocked in the womb as Mom went about her daily activities. They enjoy being rocked gently by Mom or Dad in a rocking chair. The motion is very soothing to them, and they love that bonding time.

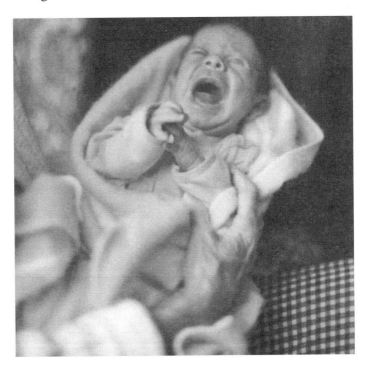

Cleaning and scrubbing
can wait 'til tomorrow,
for babies grow up we've
learned to our sorrow ...
So quiet down cobwebs,
dust go to sleep ...
I'm rocking my baby,
and babies don't keep.

Author Unknown

Baby Tips for Moms and Dads

Baby Carriers

Babies love to be carried in a baby carrier, which fits on your chest or in a sling. They are being held close to you, they hear your voice, and they are comforted by the rocking of your movements. Since newborn babies can't hold their heads up on their own yet, it is very important that your baby's head be supported and the rocking be gentle. With your baby secure in the carrier or sling, your hands are free to work.

Invest in a nice front pack. My son spent the first three months of his life in a front pack; it allowed him to spend his "fourth trimester" right where he wanted to be. It also allowed me to have my hands free, which is a luxury for a new mom.

Erica Dirksen-Queen
Mother of one

Equipment

Pacifier: To Be or Not To Be

Some parents swear by pacifiers, but I had seen too many dirty pacifiers picked up off the floor and put back in a child's mouth to risk it. I never gave either of our children one. They never knew there was such a thing and did not seem to miss it. I'm sure there were times that our children may have benefited, but I felt the problems outweighed the benefits.

Babies have great oral needs in the first six months of life, and pacifiers or a thumb easily fill the bill. The downside is that pacifiers are easily abused. Pacifiers can lead to sleep problems because it becomes a crutch to help the infant fall asleep. Then the baby awakens in the night and needs this crutch to go back to sleep. Later, weaning your child from the pacifier can cause more stress than the benefits gained.

Parents start out with the best of intentions, but the pacifier easily becomes the automatic response to any whimper or sign of discomfort. You need first to seek the cause of the discomfort.

Baby Tips for Moms and Dads

If you do use a pacifier to help your child with strong sucking needs, use it in moderation. A pacifier is a hard habit to break.

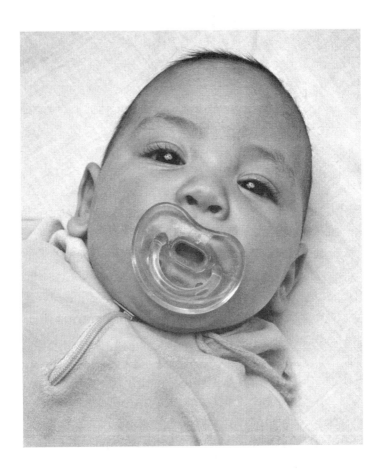

The simplest toy, one which even the youngest child can operate, is called a grandparent.

Sam Levenson (1911–1980)

Humorist

Baby Tips for Moms and Dads

Swing

My children loved to swing. I would put our swing in the kitchen so that they could watch me fix dinner. They were happy in their swing watching me while I was working in the kitchen. I could talk to them and wind up the swing for another round as I got dinner on the table.

Vaporizers

Vaporizers are used for upper respiratory infections and other illnesses such as croup, bronchitis, and pneumonia. A simple cool mist vaporizer spews out large particles (not a fine mist) of water. This is all that is necessary. Constant use is not necessary; you just want to increase the vaporization in the room. Your vaporizer must be cleaned daily to prevent mold. And be careful: Hot or warm mist vaporizers greatly increase the risk of burns.

Playpen

This is the best invention for a safe play area for an inquisitive baby when Mom or Dad need to get a little work done.

Equipment

Our children loved to spend time in their playpen. Our son would pull himself up to the rail and watch me prepare a meal. He would often fall asleep and take a nap there as well. It wasn't long until my son could throw one leg over the rail and out he would go. In order to turn my back for a few minutes, I had to go to Plan B. My husband was a contractor, so building supplies were handy. First I added a sheet of plywood to the top of the playpen. When our son pushed that aside, I had to add a cinder block. This sounds cruel but before my son could walk he would pull out the bank of drawers in the kitchen to make stairsteps to the kitchen counter. Now our son is a contractor like his dad and a new father. We'll see how he handles this playpen time for his child.

MQ

PLAYTIME

Play

Babies love for you to play with them. They will smile at a simple peek-a-boo, a funny noise, a tickle with your finger. Put on some music and dance around the room with them. They will enjoy this fun interaction with their parents.

As they become older and more mobile, your children will need safe play areas where they can experiment with their environment. A fenced-in yard is a good beginning. Children need places where they can run, climb on things, play in the sprinkler, and dig in the dirt.

Take time to see the world through their eyes and play, play, play with them.

Judy Garrett

Mother of three, grandmother of ten

Baby Tips for Moms and Dads

People joke about kids leaving the toys alone and playing with the boxes. It's true that small children love boxes. Get some large boxes from the appliance store. Cut windows in them, leaving one side so it will swing. Cut out doors. Paint shutters on the windows. Cover chairs with sheets and make awnings. Use tape to make additional roofs. All this costs very little and your kids will love a little house of their own.

Jack Queen

Father of two, grandfather of one

You may want to join a play group where your children can play with others their age. Mom or Dad will enjoy a chance to visit while the children are playing together. Toddlers often will play near each other but not with each other. It takes some time to develop the social skills necessary for understanding about sharing space and toys.

Playtime

My favorite place as a child was a large sandbox. All I needed was a bucket of water, a digging tool, and a few toys. I would play for hours here. We would dig tunnels and make all kind of shapes with the wet sand. As I got older, projects in the big sandbox became an entire neighborhood event. If you have cats you should have a lid for the sandbox when not in use.

MQ

Vacationing with Your Baby

Long drives in the car are difficult with small children. They are confined to their carseat, which is frustrating for an active child. One parent should read stories and play games—everyone can sing along to music in the car. Bring snacks for the entire family. Everyone will be happier if the drive time is short.

Play is often talked about as if it were a relief from serious learning. But for children, play is serious learning. Play is really the work of childhood.

Fred Rogers (1928–2003)

Creator of the "Mr. Rogers' Neighborhood" children's television show

Playtime

Our best vacations with little children were camping at our local state park, which had a beautiful beach. Our children would spend hours playing in the sand. They would climb up the sand banks and jump off, crashing down harmlessly in an avalanche of sand. We could enjoy talking to each other as we watched our children at play. Our family would walk along the beach together picking up shells. As a family, we watched sunsets together, listened to the waves together, lay on our backs and counted the stars together. This was a bonding experience for all of us, and a weekend we could often afford.

MQ

Baby Tips for Moms and Dads

What about TV time?

My recommendation is to keep television watching at a minimum.

Don't consider the television as a babysitting tool. Entertain your children by reading to them and creating an interest in the wonderful stories that books contain.

Monitor the television shows that your children watch for violence as well as sexual content.

Music

Children love listening to music. Our daughter began to dance to music almost as soon as she could walk. Music and singing are great entertainment when riding in the car as well. You'll find a huge selection of children's songs available on CDs.

Children have never been very good at listening to their elders but have never failed to imitate them.

James Baldwin (1924–1987)

Writer

CHILDCARE

Babysitters

Picking a good babysitter is so important. This is one place you can't be too careful. Get recommendations from your friends. Your church is also a good place to find a babysitter. Get references; talk to others whom this person has sat for. Have the prospective babysitter come to your house and spend an evening with your child while you are at home. This will give you a chance to see how your child interacts with this person, and the babysitter can become familiar with your household as well.

Day Care

If you are planning on returning to work, picking out a good day care facility is important. Drop by to check out the facility unannounced. Are the children actively involved in activities? Are they supervised properly? What food does the day care serve? Is the facility clean? (Look in a closet or the kitchen.) Do the children seem happy? What is the child-to-caregiver ratio?

Go Back to Work or Stay Home?

This is one of the hardest decisions a parent has to make. One way to compromise is for one parent to work from home. You can be a writer, editor, consultant, sales rep, sell Tupperware, or even have an eBay sales business from home. You can't do this full-time, but you can work part-time from home. This saves the cost of day care, and you get to spend some quality time with your child every day.

If you are a stay-at-home mom or dad, get together with friends who also are at home with their children. Plan outings to the park or other locations where you can visit with your friends and watch your children play at the same time. This gives you some social contact with other moms or dads and gets everyone out of the house.

Your children need your presence more than your presents.

Jessie Jackson (1941–)
Religious leader and political activist

FINAL THOUGHTS

I have given lists of tips to help you along the parenting path. All of this advice can be summed up with the following recipe for healthy, happy children.

1. Let them grow up in an atmosphere of love, patience, and kindness.

2. Promote good, healthy eating habits.

3. Make sure your children get enough sleep.

4. Provide a safe living and playing environment.

5. Give your children reasonable family rules and expectations.

6. Establish a general daily routine.

Baby Tips for Moms and Dads

Children Learn What They Live

If a child lives with criticism,
He learns to condemn.
If a child lives with hostility,
He learns to fight.
If a child lives with ridicule,
He learns to be shy.
If a child lives with shame,
He learns to feel guilty.
If a child lives with tolerance,
He learns to be patient.
If a child lives with encouragement,
He learns confidence.
If a child lives with praise,
He learns to appreciate.
If a child lives with fairness,
He learns justice.
If a child lives with security,
He learns to have faith.
If a child lives with approval,
He learns to like himself.
If a child lives with acceptance and
    friendship,
He learns to find love in the world.

Dorothy Law Nolte, Educator and writer

My Favorite Words of Wisdom about Children

One hundred years from now, it will not matter what my bank account was, the sort of house that I lived in, or what kind of car I drove. But the world may be a little different because I was important in the life of a boy.

Forest Witcraft (1894–1967)

Scholar, teacher, Boy Scout leader

Baby Tips for Moms and Dads

My Favorite Reference Book

What To Expect the First Year by Heidi Murkoff, Arlene Eisenberg & Sandee Hathaway B.S.N. New York. Workman Publishing 2003.

Websites for Information

1. La Leche League International
   www.lalecheleague.org

2. American Academy of Pediatrics
   www.aap.org

3. American Medical Association
   www.ama-assn.org

Live so that when your children think of fairness and integrity, they think of you.

H. Jackson Brown (1940–)
Author of *Life's Little Instruction Book*

Index

Index

Baby Tips for Moms and Dads

Index

ABOUT THE AUTHOR

Margaret Queen has worked with children as a teacher and camp counselor for more than twenty years. She has a master of arts degree from the University of California, Santa Barbara. Margaret has two grown children and one grandchild. She lives with her husband in Tennessee.

Margaret Queen and her father